Mix and Match

Crochet Animals

Amigurumi Crochet Patterns

Sayjai Thawornsupacharoen

Mix and Match series, volume 1

K AND J PUBLISHING
16 Whitegate Close, Swavesey, Cambridge CB24 4TT, England
kandjdolls.blogspot.com / www.facebook.com/kandjdolls.amigurumi.patterns

CONTENTS

INTRODUCTION

Mix and Match series

Welcome to the first crochet pattern book in the Mix and Match series, in which you can mix and match a whole range of animals (head patterns) and costumes (body patterns) to your heart's content. Everything from the mighty elephant to a nimble mouse is encompassed in these patterns, and your child will love playing with your very own costumed creations. They also make for adorable gifts for loved ones, and changing them up is a piece of cake! Just switch up the yarn thickness and hook size to upsize or downsize your teddy, or pull out the accessories and cute yarn colours and let your creativity flow. Soon enough your yarn could become the ballerina cow you've always dreamt of.

Bear family

Mr and Mrs Bear are made from Worsted weight yarn and a 4 mm hook.

Head : Bear, see page 35.
Body : Mr Bear : doctor, see page 44.
Mrs Bear : nurse, see page 46.

Girl and Boy Bear are made from DK yarn and a 3 mm hook.

Head : Bear, see page 35.
Body : Girl Bear, same as nurse on page 46.
Boy Bear, same as engineer on page 60.

About Sayjai

Sayjai is a former nurse and self-taught Amigurumi crocheter who started designing Amigurumi crochet patterns in 2009. She opened her shop on Etsy (K and J Dolls) selling her original designed Amigurumi crochet patterns, and by 2014 had written her first published pattern book. Throughout the years Sayjai's original designs have featured in crochet magazines like Let's Knit and Trendy Häkeln and in books like Witch Craft and Dress Up Dolls.

Thank you for supporting an independent designer.
Write to Sayjai : kandjdolls@gmail.com
kandjdolls.blogspot.com / www.facebook.com/kandjdolls.amigurumi.patterns

BEAR

PIG

ELEPHANT

TIGER

COW

MOUSE

MONKEY

DOCTOR

CHEF

POLICE

FARMER

BALLERINA

ENGINEER

MATERIALS

Size

The size of the animal depends on the size of the crochet hook, the thickness of yarn and how you stuff it; a bigger hook and thicker yarn make a bigger animal. A tightly stuffed animal is bigger than a lightly stuffed one.

On the left are three sizes: the small teddy bear was made with DK yarn and a 3 mm hook, the medium sized bear was made from Worsted (Aran) yarn and a 4 mm hook and the large teddy bear was made from Chunky yarn and a 5 mm hook.

Finished Size	Yarn weight	Yarn Quantity		Hook Size	Safety eyes	Polyester fiberfill
		Head	Body			
Large 11 inches/ 28 cm tall (excluding ears)	**5** Bulky — Bulky, Chunky yarn	35-60 g (1.2-2.1 oz) or 50-86 metres (55-94 yds)	50-85 g (1.8-3 oz) or 72-122 metres (79-133 yds)	5 mm hook, H/8	15 mm safety eyes	250 g
Medium 8.5 inches/ 22 cm tall (excluding ears)	**4** Medium — Aran, Worsted weight yarn	30-50 g (1.1-1.8 oz) or 49-82 metres (54-90 yds)	50-70 g (1.8-2.5 oz) or 82-115 metres (90-126 yds)	4 mm hook, G/6	12 mm safety eyes	70 g
Small 6.5 inches/ 17 cm tall (excluding ears)	**3** Light — DK, Light worsted yarn	10-20 g (0.4-0.7 oz) or 29.5-59 metres (32-65 yds)	15-20 g (0.5-0.7 oz) or 44-59 metres (48-65 yds)	3 mm hook	9 mm safety eyes	50 g

You can use the following yarn brands:

- Large size: Bulky, Chunky yarn : Stylecraft Special Chunky, ball weight 100g (3.5oz), length 144m (157yds)
- Medium size: Aran, Worsted weight yarn : Red Heart Soft Yarn, ball weight 100g (3.5oz), length 167m (183yds) and Red Heart Soft Baby Steps Yarn, ball weight 100g (3.5oz), length 164m (179yds)
- Small size: DK, Light worsted yarn : Stylecraft Special DK, ball weight 100g (3.5oz), length 295m (323yds)

Yarn for the medium sized dolls:

BLACK TEXT : Red Heart Soft Yarn, **PINK TEXT** : Red Heart Soft Baby Steps Yarn

Ice Blue (00008)	Light Yellow (00002)	Light Pink (00003)	Orange (00003)	Grey (00012)
White (00001)	White (00001)	Really Red (09925)	Marine (00006)	Really Red (09925)
Wheat (09388)	Nature (00002)	Black (00014)	Black (00014)	Black (00014)
Nature (00002)		White (00001)	Yellow (08217)	Yellow (08217)
			White (00001)	

Wheat (09388)	White (00001)	Grey (00012)	Wheat (09388)	White (00001)
White (00001)	Black (00014)	White (00001)	Marine (00006)	Light Pink (00003)
Black (00014)	Light Pink (00003)	Light Pink (00003)	Light Blue (00007)	Grey (00012)
Marine (00006)	Marine (00006)	Nature (00002)	Nature (00002)	Strawberry (00004)
Brown (08281)	Orange (00003)		Yellow (08217)	
	Brown (08281)		Black (00014)	

Embroidery thread

Black embroidery floss (DMC Pearl Cotton Thread Size 5) is used to embroider the nose, eye lashes and mouth.

Other equipment

- Tapestry needle or needle with a big eyelet.
- Stitch marker or a piece of yarn for marking the beginning of the round.
- Pins are used for keeping ears, arms and feet in place.
- A small pair of pointed scissors. You can use the tip of the scissors to push the stuffing into a small part of the doll or to make a hole for inserting the safety eyes.

Other decorative items

You can decorate your animals with ribbons, small buttons, beads and other accessories.

BASIC STITCHES

Crochet Stitches Used

- single crochet (UK: double crochet)
- half double crochet (UK: half treble crochet)
- double crochet (UK: treble crochet)
- slip stitch
- chain

Abbreviations

This book uses US crochet terms.

ch = chain
sc = single crochet
hdc = half double crochet
dc = double crochet
st = stitch
sl = slip
rnd = round
tog = together

Conversion chart for USA/ UK crochet terms

USA	UK
sc = single crochet	dc = double crochet
hdc = half double crochet	htr = half treble crochet
dc = double crochet	tr = treble crochet

Slip Knot

Chain Stitch (ch)

Yarn over the hook and pull it through the loop. The first chain is made.

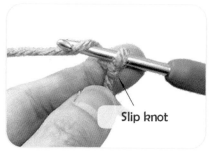

Slip knot

one chain made

Single Crochet (sc)

1) Insert the hook into next stitch (or chain),
2) yarn over, pull yarn through the stitch (or chain).
3) You will have 2 loops on the hook,
4) yarn over and pull the yarn through both loops on the hook.
5) One single crochet (sc) is made.

Half Double Crochet (hdc)

1) Yarn over,
2) insert the hook into next stitch (or chain), yarn over, pull yarn through the stitch (or chain).
3) You will have 3 loops on the hook, yarn over and pull the yarn through all 3 loops.
4) One half double crochet is made.

Double Crochet (dc)

1) Yarn over,
2) insert the hook into next stitch (or chain), yarn over, pull yarn through the stitch (or chain).
3) You will have 3 loops on the hook, yarn over and pull the yarn through 2 loops on the hook.
4) You will have 2 loops on the hook, yarn over and pull the yarn through 2 loops on the hook.
5) One double crochet is made.

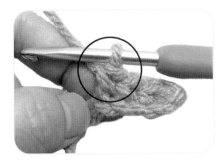
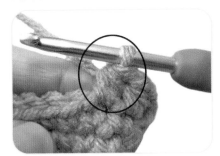

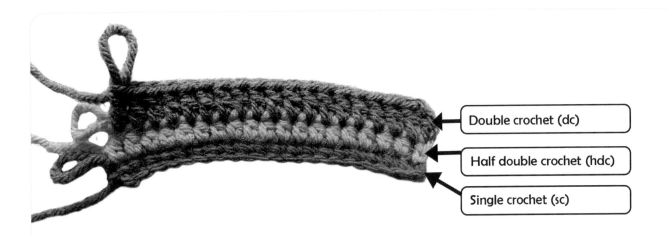

Double crochet (dc)

Half double crochet (hdc)

Single crochet (sc)

Continuous Rounds (Spirals)

Working in continuous rounds is when you come to the end of the round, you crochet into the first stitch of the previous round and keep going. It is useful to mark the first stitch of each round with a stitch marker or a piece of yarn. Because it will be difficult to identify where the round begins or ends.

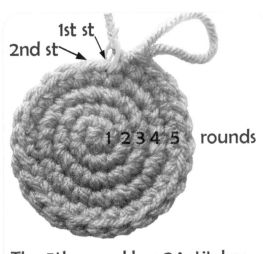

1st st
2nd st
1 2 3 4 5 rounds

The 5th round has 24 stitches.

Single Crochet Increase (2 single crochet in same stitch)

1) Insert the hook into next stitch (or chain), yarn over, pull yarn through the stitch (or chain).
2) You will have 2 loops on the hook, yarn over and pull the yarn through both loops on the hook,
3) the first sc is made.
4) Insert the hook into same stitch (or chain), yarn over, pull yarn through the stitch (or chain).
5) You will have 2 loops on the hook, yarn over and pull the yarn through both loops on the hook,
6) the second sc is made.

Single Crochet Decrease (single crochet next 2 stitches together)

1) Insert the hook into next stitch (or chain), yarn over, pull yarn through the stitch (or chain).

2) You will have 2 loops on the hook,

3) insert the hook into next stitch, yarn over and pull the yarn through the stitch.

4) You will have 3 loops on the hook,

5) yarn over the hook and pull through 3 loops on the hook.

6) Single crochet decrease made ("Sc next 2 sts tog").

Back Loops

To work in the back loop of a stitch, insert your hook underneath the back loop only and make the stitch as indicated in the pattern.

The pictures below show working single crochet in back loops only.

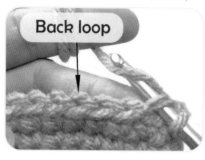

You will see free loops in the front (right side).

Front Loops

To work in the front loop of a stitch, insert your hook underneath the front loop only and make the stitch as indicated in the pattern.

The pictures below show working single crochet in front loops only.

You will see free loops in the back (wrong side).

Magic Ring Foundation

The head and many parts start with a Magic Ring. You begin with an adjustable ring and then crochet the rows or rounds of your project on top of this ring. The finished piece will be a circle or spherical shape.

Basic Magic Ring

1) Put the yarn end behind the yarn from the ball/ skein to make a loop.

2) Put the hook through the loop and yarn over the hook. Pull the yarn through the loop.

3) The ring is made.

28

Rnd 1: Crochet 6 sc in a magic
ring.

1) First make a Basic Magic Ring
(see previous page), insert hook
through the Magic Ring, yarn over,
pull through the ring.

2) You will have 2 loops on the
hook.

3) Yarn over, pull through both
loops on the hook.

4) One single crochet is made.

5) Repeat five times more, until 6
single crochet stitches are made
and pull the yarn end to close the
ring.

Foundation Chain

Sometimes an Amigurumi doll is starting from chains and you will crochet
the rows or rounds of your project on top of these chains. This will create
an oval, square or rectangular shape.

Rnd 1: Ch 12, sc in second chain from hook, sc in next 9 chs, 3 sc in next
ch; working in remaining loops on opposite side of chain, sc in next 9 chs,
2 sc in next ch. (24 sts made)

The colors in the diagram below are the same colors as in the above
instructions.

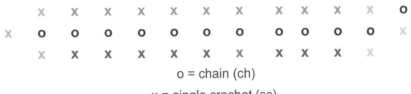

o = chain (ch)

x = single crochet (sc)

1) Make 12 chains.

2) Sc in second chain from hook.

3) Sc in next 9 chains.

4) 3 sc in next chain.

5) Working in remaining loops on
opposite side of chain, sc in next
9 chs.

6) 2 sc in next chain. (24)

BASIC PATTERNS

Collar

Working in rows.

Row 1: Ch 25, dc in 4th ch from hook (first 3 chs count as 1 dc), hdc in next ch, sc in next 18 chs, hdc in next ch, 2 dc in next ch, leave long end for sewing, fasten off. (24)

Wrap collar around the neck and sew.

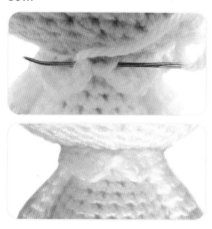

Muzzle

Rnd 1: 6 sc in a magic ring. (6)

Rnd 2: (2 sc in next st, sc in next st) 3 times, sl st in first st, leave long end for sewing, fasten off. (9)

With **BLACK** embroidery floss, embroider nose.

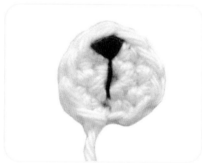

Belt

Working in rows.

Row 1: Ch 36, sc in second ch from hook, sc in next 34 chs, leave long end for sewing, fasten off. (35)

Sew belt on rnds 5-6 of the body, with **YELLOW YARN** embroider a buckle as in pictures below.

Head

Rnd 1: 6 sc in a magic ring. (6)

Rnd 2: 2 sc in each st around. (12)

Rnd 3: (Sc in next st, 2 sc in next st) 6 times. (18)

Rnd 4: (2 sc in next st, sc in next 2 sts) 6 times. (24)

Rnd 5: (Sc in next 3 sts, 2 sc in next st) 6 times. (30)

Rnd 6: Sc in next 2 sts, 2 sc in next st, (sc in next 4 sts, 2 sc in next st) 5 times, sc in next 2 sts. (36)

Rnd 7: (Sc in next 5 sts, 2 sc in next st) 6 times. (42)

Rnd 8: Sc in next 3 sts, 2 sc in next st, (sc in next 6 sts, 2 sc in next st) 5 times, sc in next 3 sts. (48)

Rnd 9: (Sc in next 7 sts, 2 sc in next st) 6 times. (54)

Rnd 10-16: Sc in each st around. (54)

Rnd 17: (Sc in next 7 sts, sc next 2 sts tog) 6 times. (48)

Rnd 18: Sc in next 3 sts, sc next 2 sts tog, (sc in next 6 sts, sc next 2 sts tog) 5 times, sc in next 3 sts. (42)

Rnd 19: (Sc in next 5 sts, sc next 2 sts tog) 6 times. (36)

Rnd 20: Sc in next 2 sts, sc next 2 sts tog, (sc in next 4 sts, sc next 2 sts tog) 5 times, sc in next 2 sts. (30)

Rnd 21: (Sc in next 3 sts, sc next 2 sts tog) 6 times. (24)

Insert safety eyes 7-8 sts apart between rnds 14-15.

Rnd 22: (Sc in next 2 sts, sc next 2 sts tog) 6 times. (18)

Rnd 23: (Sc in next st, sc next 2 sts tog) 6 times, sl st to the first st, fasten off. (12) Stuff head.

If the stitches are very tight use the tip of small scissors to make holes for inserting the safety eyes.

How to connect the legs together
Diagram for how to connect the legs together.

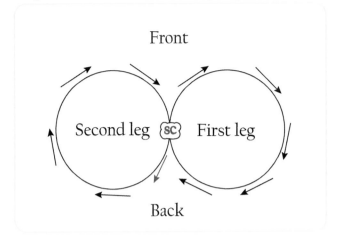

Front

Second leg **sc** First leg

Back

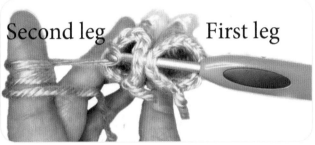

Second leg   First leg

31

Tail

Ch 10, leave long end for sewing, fasten off. (10 chs)

Hair at the end of tail: Cut 1-2 pieces of yarn 2" (5 cm) long. Hold one strand of yarn, fold in half, insert hook through the end of tail, draw the folded end through the stitch and pull the loose ends through the folded end, draw the knot up tightly. Use a needle to split the yarns to make them fluffy.

Sew tail on rnd 5 or 6, middle back of the body.

Working in free loops

For skirt or the edge of shirt.

Sew arms to the body

Position arms as in the picture below and sew through both arms and body.

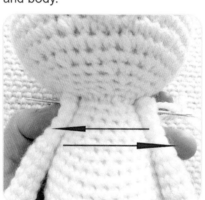

Eyelashes

With **BLACK** embroidery floss, embroider the eyelashes.

Mr Elephant

Made from Worsted weight yarn and a 4 mm hook.

Head : Elephant,
see page 38.

Body: Firefighter,
see page 52.

Girl Elephant

Made from DK yarn and a 3 mm hook.

Head : Elephant,
see page 38.

Body: Same as the ballerina on page 58.

Mrs Elephant

Made from Worsted weight yarn and a 4 mm hook.

Head : Elephant,
see page 38.

Body: Nurse, see page 46.

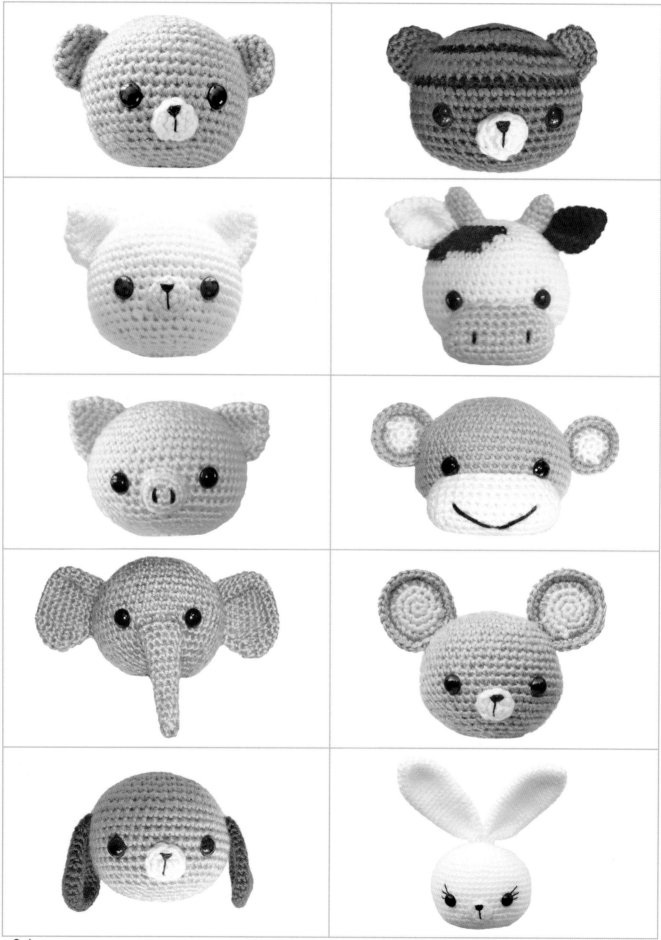

BEAR

Head

BROWN, see page 31.

Ear

Make 2.

Rnd 1: With **BROWN**, 6 sc in a magic ring. (6)

Rnd 2: 2 sc in each st around. (12)

Rnd 3: (2 sc in next st, sc in next 3 sts) 3 times. (15)

Rnd 4: Sc in each st around. (15)

Rnd 5: Sc in each st around, sl st to the first st, leave long end for sewing, fasten off. (15)
Pin ears on rnds 7-12 of head and sew.

Muzzle

CREAM, see page 30.
Pin muzzle on rnds 15-18 and sew.

CAT

Head

YELLOW, see page 31.

Ear

Make 2.

Rnd 1: With **YELLOW**, 4 sc in a magic ring. (4)

Rnd 2: (Sc in next st, 2 sc in next st) 2 times. (6)

Rnd 3: 2 sc in each st around. (12)

Rnd 4: (Sc in next 3 sts, 2 sc in next st) 3 times. (15)

Rnd 5: Sc in each st around. (15)

Rnd 6: Sc in each st around, sl st to the first st, leave long end for sewing, fasten off. (15)
Pin ears on rnds 7-12 of head and sew.

Muzzle

CREAM, see page 30.
Pin muzzle on rnds 14-17 and sew.

Tail

Rnd 1: With **YELLOW**, 4 sc in a magic ring. (4)

Rnd 2-14: Sc in each st around. (4)

Rnd 15: Sc in each st around, sl st to the first st, leave long end for sewing, fasten off. (4)
Sew tail on rnds 6-7 of the body.

TIGER

Head

Use **BLACK** for the black stripes where the text is **PINK**.
Use **ORANGE** where the text is **BLACK**.

Rnd 1: 6 sc in a magic ring. (6)

Rnd 2: 2 sc in each st around. (12)

Rnd 3: (Sc in next st, 2 sc in next st) 6 times. (18)

Rnd 4: (2 sc in next st, sc in next 2 sts) 6 times. (24)

Rnd 5: (Sc in next 3 sts, 2 sc in next st) 6 times. (30)

Rnd 6: Sc in next 2 sts, 2 sc in next st, (sc in next 4 sts, 2 sc in next st) 5 times, sc in next 2 sts. (36)

Rnd 7: (Sc in next 5 sts, 2 sc in next st) 6 times. (42)

Rnd 8: Sc in next 3 sts, 2 sc in next st, (sc in next 6 sts, 2 sc in next st) 5 times, sc in next 3 sts. (48)

Rnd 9: (Sc in next 7 sts, 2 sc in next st) 6 times. (54)

Rnd 10: Sc in each st around. (54)

Rnd 11: Sc in each st around. (54)

Rnd 12-13: Sc in each st around. (54)

Rnd 14: Sc in next 10 sts, sc in next 20 sts, sc in next 24 sts. (54)

Rnd 15-16: Sc in each st around. (54)

Rnd 17: Sc in next 7 sts, sc next 2 sts tog, sc in next 2 sts, sc in next 5 sts, sc next 2 sts tog, sc in next 7 sts, sc next 2 sts tog, sc in next 4 sts, sc in next 3 sts, sc next 2 sts tog, (sc in next 7 sts, sc next 2 sts tog) 2 times. (48)

Rnd 18: Sc in next 3 sts, sc next 2 sts tog, (sc in next 6 sts, sc next 2 sts tog) 5 times, sc in next 3 sts. (42)

Rnd 19: (Sc in next 5 sts, sc next 2 sts tog) 6 times. (36)

Rnd 20: Sc in next 2 sts, sc next 2 sts tog, sc in next 4 sts, sc next 2 sts tog, (sc in next 4 sts, sc next 2 sts tog) 2 times, (sc in next 4 sts, sc next 2 sts tog) 2 times, sc in next 2 sts. (30)

Rnd 21: (Sc in next 3 sts, sc next 2 sts tog) 6 times. (24)

Insert safety eyes 7-8 sts apart between rnds 14-15.

Rnd 22: (Sc in next 2 sts, sc next 2 sts tog) 6 times. (18)

Rnd 23: (Sc in next st, sc next 2 sts tog) 6 times, sl st to the first st, leave long end for sewing, fasten off. (12)

Stuff head tightly by using tip of scissors to push the stuffing in.

Ear

Make 2.

Rnd 1: With **ORANGE**, 6 sc in a magic ring. (6)

Rnd 2: 2 sc in each st around. (12)

Rnd 3-4: Sc in each st around. (12)

Rnd 5: Sc in each st around, sl st to the first st, leave long end for sewing, fasten off. (12)

Pin ears on rnds 7-11 of head and sew.

Muzzle

WHITE, see page 30.

Pin muzzle on rnds 14-17 and sew.

Tail

Use **BLACK (STRIPES COLOR)** where text is **PINK**.
Use **ORANGE** where text is **BLACK**.

Rnd 1: 4 sc in a magic ring. (4)

Rnd 2-4: Sc in each st around. (4)

Rnd 5-6: Sc in each st around. (4)

Rnd 7: Sc in each st around. (4)

Rnd 8-9: Sc in each st around. (4)

Rnd 10: Sc in each st around. (4)

Rnd 11-12: Sc in each st around. (4)

Rnd 13: Sc in each st around. (4)

Rnd 14: Sc in each st around. (4)

Rnd 15: Sc in each st around, sl st to the first st, leave long end for sewing, fasten off. (4)

Sew tail on rnd 5-6 of the body.

PIG

Head

LIGHT PINK, see page 31.

Ear

Make 2.

Rnd 1: With **LIGHT PINK**, 4 sc in a magic ring. (4)

Rnd 2: (Sc in next st, 2 sc in next st) 2 times. (6)

Rnd 3: 2 sc in each st around. (12)

Rnd 4: (Sc in next 3 sts, 2 sc in next st) 3 times. (15)

Rnd 5: Sc in each st around. (15)

Rnd 6: Sc in each st around, sl st to the first st, leave long end for sewing, fasten off. (15)

Pin ears on rnds 6-12 of head and sew.

Tail

Working in rows.

Row 1: With **LIGHT PINK**, ch 10, 2 sl st in second ch from hook, 2 sl st in next 8 chs, leave long end for sewing, fasten off. (18)

Sew tail on rnd 6 of the body.

Snout

Start by crocheting sc around the foundation chain:

Rnd 1: With **LIGHT PINK**, ch 3, sc in second chain from hook, 3 sc in next ch; working in remaining loops on opposite side of chain, 2 sc in next ch. (6)

```
        x   x   o
    x   o   o   x
        x   x
```

o = chain, x = single crochet

Rnd 2: 2 sc in each st around. (12)

Rnd 3: Working in back loops only. Sc in each st around, sl st in first st, leave long end for sewing, fasten off. (12)

With **BLACK YARN**, embroider 2 lines on snout.

Pin snout on rnds 14-16 between the eyes and sew it to head, stuff snout before sewing the opening closed.

ELEPHANT

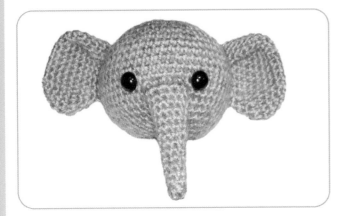

Head

GREY, see page 31.

Ear

Make 2.

Start by crocheting sc around the foundation chain:

Rnd 1: With **GREY**, ch 7, sc in second chain from hook, sc in next 4 chs, 3 sc in last ch; working in remaining loops on opposite side of chain, sc in next 4 chs, 2 sc in next ch. (14)

```
        x   x   x   x   x   x   o
    x   o   o   o   o   o   o   x
        x   x   x   x   x   x
```

o = chain, x = single crochet

Rnd 2: 2 sc in next st, sc in next 4 sts, 2 sc in next 3 sts, sc in next 4 sts, 2 sc in next 2 sts. (20)

Rnd 3: Sc in next st, 2 sc in next st, sc in next 5 sts, 2 sc in next st, (sc in next st, 2 sc in next st) 2 times, sc in next 5 sts, 2 sc in next st, sc in next st, 2 sc in next st. (26)

Rnd 4: Sc in next 2 sts, 2 sc in next st, sc in next 6 sts, 2 sc in next st, (sc in next 2 sts, 2 sc in next st) 2 times, sc in next 6 sts, 2 sc in next st, sc in next 2 sts, 2 sc in next st. (32)

Rnd 5: Sc in each st around. (32)

Rnd 6: Sc in next 10 sts, (sc next 2 sts tog) 5 times, sc in next 12 sts. (27)

Rnd 7: Sc in each st around. (27)

Rnd 8: Sc in next 9 sts, (sc next 2 sts tog) 4 times, sc in next 10 sts. (23)

Rnd 9: Sc in each st around, sl st in first st, leave long end for sewing, fasten off. (23)

Fold the top of the ear about 3 sts and sew.

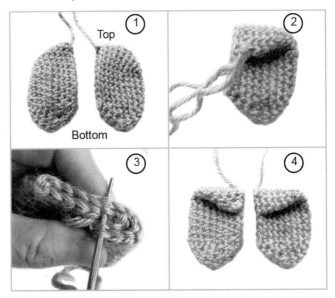

Pin ears on rnds 8-14 of head and sew.

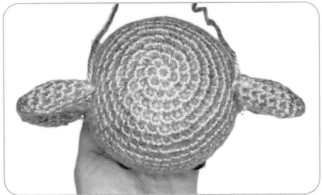

Trunk

Rnd 1: With **GREY**, 6 sc in a magic ring. (6)

Rnd 2: Working in back loops only. Sc in each st around. (6)

Rnd 3: 2 sc in next st, sc in next 5 sts. (7)

Rnd 4-5: Sc in each st around. (7)

Rnd 6: 2 sc in next st, sc in next 6 sts. (8)

Rnd 7-8: Sc in each st around. (8)

Rnd 9: 2 sc in next st, sc in next 7 sts. (9)

Rnd 10-11: Sc in each st around. (9)

Rnd 12: 2 sc in next st, sc in next 8 sts. (10)

Rnd 13-14: Sc in each st around. (10)

Rnd 15: Sc in next 4 sts, 2 sc in next 3 sts, sc in next 3 sts, sl st in first st, leave long end for sewing, fasten off. (13)

Do not stuff trunk, flatten the last round and sew the opening closed with the end of rnd in the middle as in the picture below.

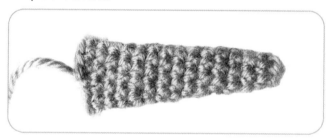

Pin trunk on rnds 15-18 and sew.

Tail

GREY, see page 32.

DOG

Head

BROWN, see page 31.

Ear

Rnd 1: With **DARK BROWN**, 6 sc in a magic ring. (6)

Rnd 2: 2 sc in each st around. (12)

Rnd 3: (Sc in next st, 2 sc in next st) 6 times. (18)

Rnd 4: (2 sc in next st, sc in next 2 sts) 6 times. (24)

Rnd 5-7: Sc in each st around. (24)

Rnd 8: (Sc in next 2 sts, sc next 2 sts tog) 6 times. (18)

Rnd 9-11: Sc in each st around. (18)

Rnd 12: (Sc next 2 sts tog, sc in next 4 sts) 3 times. (15)

Rnd 13: Sc in each st around. (15)

Rnd 14: (Sc in next 3 sts, sc next 2 sts tog) 3 times. (12)

Rnd 15: Sc in each st around. (12)

Rnd 16: Sc in each st around, join with sl st in first st. Leave long end for sewing, fasten off. (12)

Pin ears on rnd 11 of head and sew.

Muzzle

CREAM, see page 30.

Pin muzzle on rnds 15-18 and sew.

RABBIT

Head

WHITE, see page 31.

Muzzle

WHITE, see page 30.
Sew muzzle on rnds 14-17.

Eyelashes

With **BLACK** embroidery floss, embroider eyelashes (see page 32).

Ear

Make 2.

Rnd 1: With **WHITE**, 6 sc in a magic ring. (6)

Rnd 2: (Sc in next st, 2 sc in next st) 3 times. (9)

Rnd 3: (Sc in next 2 sts, 2 sc in next st) 3 times. (12)

Rnd 4: (Sc in next 3 sts, 2 sc in next st) 3 times. (15)

Rnd 5: (Sc in next 4 sts, 2 sc in next st) 3 times. (18)

Rnd 6-15: Sc in each st around. (18)

Rnd 16: (Sc next 2 sts tog, sc in next 4 sts) 3 times. (15)

Rnd 17-19: Sc in each st around. (15)

Rnd 20: (Sc next 2 sts tog, sc in next 3 sts) 3 times. (12)

Rnd 21-22: Sc in each st around. (12)

Rnd 23: Sc in each st around, join with sl st in first st. Leave long end for sewing, fasten off. (12)

Fold ear in half and sew the last round together.

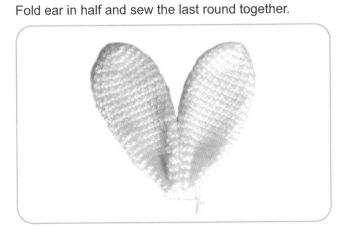

Sew ears on the middle top of the head as in the picture of the white rabbit on the left or sew ears on rnd 9 of the head as in the picture of the grey rabbit below.

MONKEY

Head

BROWN, see page 31.

Ear

Make 4 circles: 2 in **CREAM** and 2 in **BROWN**.

Rnd 1: 6 sc in a magic ring. (6)

Rnd 2: 2 sc in each st around, join with sl st in first st, fasten off. (12)

Rnd 3: Matching sts, hold one **BROWN** ear and one **CREAM** ear together. Working in rnd 2 through both thicknesses. With **CREAM** side facing you, join **BROWN** on rnd 2 with sl st, ch 1, sc in same st, 2 sc in next st, (sc in next st, 2 sc in next st) 5 times. (18)

See "How to crochet 2 pieces together" below.

Rnd 4: (2 sc in next st, sc in next 2 sts) 5 times, sl st in next st. Leave long end for sewing, fasten off. (20)

Pin ears on rnds 11-14 and sew.

How to crochet 2 pieces together

Matching sts, hold 2 pieces with wrong sides together and working through both thicknesses.

Tail

Rnd 1: With **BROWN**, 4 sc in a magic ring. (4)

Rnd 2-16: Sc in each st around. (4)

Rnd 17: Sc in each st around, sl st to the first st, leave long end for sewing, fasten off. (4)

Sew tail on rnd 5 of the body.

Muzzle

Start by crocheting sc around the foundation chain:

Rnd 1: With **CREAM**, ch 15, sc in second chain from hook, sc in next 12 chs, 3 sc in next ch; working in remaining loops on opposite side of chain, sc in next 12 chs, 2 sc in next ch. (30)

Rnd 2: 2 sc in next st, sc in next 12 sts, 2 sc in next 3 sts, sc in next 12 sts, 2 sc in next 2 sts. (36)

Rnd 3-4: Sc in each st around. (36)

Rnd 5: Sc in each st around, join with sl st in first st. Leave long end for sewing, fasten off.

Pin mouth over rnds 16-21, sew it to head and stuff before sewing the opening closed.

Mouth Use pins to mark mouth line and use **BLACK YARN** to embroider the mouth.

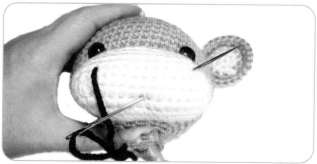

COW

Head

Use **BLACK** (PATCHES COLOR) where text is PINK.

Use **WHITE** where text is **BLACK**.

Rnd 1: 6 sc in a magic ring. (6)

Rnd 2: 2 sc in each st around. (12)

Rnd 3: (Sc in next st, 2 sc in next st) 6 times. (18)

Rnd 4: (2 sc in next st, sc in next 2 sts) 6 times. (24)

Rnd 5: (Sc in next 3 sts, 2 sc in next st) 2 times, (sc in next 3 sts, 2 sc in next st) 2 times, (sc in next 3 sts, 2 sc in next st) 2 times. (30)

Rnd 6: Sc in next 2 sts, 2 sc in next st, sc in next 4 sts, 2 sc in next st, (sc in next 4 sts, 2 sc in next st) 2 times, sc in next 2 sts, sc in next 2 sts, 2 sc in next st, sc in next 4 sts, 2 sc in next st, sc in next 2 sts. (36)

Rnd 7: Sc in next 5 sts, 2 sc in next st, sc in next 4 sts, sc in next st, 2 sc in next st, sc in next 5 sts, 2 sc in next st, sc in next 5 sts, 2 sc in next st, (sc in next 5 sts, 2 sc in next st) 2 times. (42)

Rnd 8: Sc in next 3 sts, 2 sc in next st, sc in next 6 sts, 2 sc in next st, (sc in next 6 sts, 2 sc in next st) 2 times, (sc in next 6 sts, 2 sc in next st) 2 times, sc in next 3 sts. (48)

Rnd 9: (Sc in next 7 sts, 2 sc in next st) 2 times, sc in next 7 sts, 2 sc in next st, (sc in next 7 sts, 2 sc in next st) 3 times. (54)

Rnd 10-16: Sc in each st around. (54)

Rnd 17: (Sc in next 7 sts, sc next 2 sts tog) 6 times. (48)

Rnd 18: Sc in next 3 sts, sc next 2 sts tog, (sc in next 6 sts, sc next 2 sts tog) 4 times, sc in next 3 sts, sc in next 3 sts, sc next 2 sts tog, sc in next 3 sts. (42)

Rnd 19: (Sc in next 5 sts, sc next 2 sts tog) 4 times, sc in next 5 sts, sc next 2 sts tog, sc in next 5 sts, sc next 2 sts tog. (36)

Rnd 20: Sc in next 2 sts, sc next 2 sts tog, (sc in next 4 sts, sc next 2 sts tog) 4 times, sc in next st, sc in next 3 sts, sc next 2 sts tog, sc in next 2 sts. (30)

Rnd 21: (Sc in next 3 sts, sc next 2 sts tog) 6 times. (24)

Insert safety eyes 7-8 sts apart between rnds 14-15.

Rnd 22: (Sc in next 2 sts, sc next 2 sts tog) 6 times. (18)

Rnd 23: (Sc in next st, sc next 2 sts tog) 6 times, sl st to the first st, leave long end for sewing, fasten off. (12)

Stuff head tightly by using tip of scissors to push the stuffing in.

Muzzle

Start by crocheting sc around the foundation chain:

Rnd 1: With **LIGHT PINK**, ch 12, sc in second chain from hook, sc in next 9 chs, 3 sc in next ch; working in remaining loops on opposite side of chain, sc in next 9 chs, 2 sc in next ch. (24)

o = chain, x = single crochet

Rnd 2: 2 sc in next st, sc in next 9 sts, 2 sc in next 3 sts, sc in next 9 sts, 2 sc in next 2 sts. (30)

Rnd 3-4: Sc in each st around. (30)

Rnd 5: Sc in each st around, sl st in first st, leave long end for sewing, fasten off. (30)

Pin muzzle on rnds 15-21 between the eyes and sew. Stuff before sewing the opening closed.

With **BLACK YARN**, embroider 2 lines on muzzle.

Ear

Make one in **WHITE** and one in **BLACK**.

Rnd 1: 4 sc in a magic ring. (4)

Rnd 2: (Sc in next st, 2 sc in next st) 2 times. (6)

Rnd 3: (Sc in next st, 2 sc in next st) 3 times. (9)

Rnd 4: (Sc in next 2 sts, 2 sc in next st) 3 times. (12)

Rnd 5: (Sc in next 3 sts, 2 sc in next st) 3 times. (15)

Rnd 6-7: Sc in each st around. (15)

Rnd 8: (Sc next 2 sts tog) 6 times, sc in next 3 sts. (9)

Rnd 9: (Sc next 2 sts tog) 3 times, sc in next 3 sts, sl st to the first st, leave long end for sewing, fasten off. (6)

Fold ears in half and sew on rnd 6 of head.

Horn

Rnd 1: With **LIGHT PINK**, 6 sc in a magic ring. (6)

Rnd 2: 2 sc in next st, sc in next 5 sts. (7)

Rnd 3: Sc in next 6 sts, 2 sc in next st. (8)

Rnd 4: 2 sc in next st, sc in next 7 sts. (9)

Rnd 5: Sc in next 8 sts, 2 sc in next st, sl st in first st, leave long end for sewing, fasten off. (10)

Pin horns on rnds 3-5 and sew, stuff before sewing the opening closed.

Tail

WHITE, see page 32.

Sew tail on rnd 6 of the body.

Eyelashes

With **BLACK EMBROIDERY FLOSS**, embroider eyelashes (see page 32).

Head

GREY, see page 31.

Ear

Make 4 circles: 2 in **GREY** and 2 in **LIGHT PINK**.

Rnd 1: 6 sc in a magic ring. (6)

Rnd 2: 2 sc in each st around. (12)

Rnd 3: (2 sc in next st, sc in next st) 6 times, join with sl st in first st, fasten off. (18)

Rnd 4: Matching sts, hold one **PINK** ear and one **GREY** ear together. Working in rnd 3 through both thicknesses. With **LIGHT PINK** side facing you, join **GREY** on rnd 3 with sl st, ch 1, sc in same st, 2 sc in next st, (sc in next 2 sts, 2 sc in next st) 5 times, sc in next st. (24)

See how to crochet 2 pieces together on page 41.

Rnd 5: (Sc in next 3 sts, 2 sc in next st) 5 times, sc in next st, sl st in next st, leave long end for sewing, fasten off. (28)

Pin ears on rnds 6-9 of head and sew.

Muzzle

CREAM, see page 30.

Sew muzzle on rnds 14-17.

Tail

With **GREY**, ch 20, sl st in second ch from hook, sl st in next 18 chs, leave long end for sewing, fasten off. (19)

Sew tail on rnd 6 of the body.

43

DOCTOR

Leg

Make 2.

Start by crocheting sc around the foundation chain:

Rnd 1: With **WHITE**, ch 5, sc in second chain from hook, sc in next 2 chs, 3 sc in last ch; working in remaining loops on opposite side of chain, sc in next 2 chs, 2 sc in next ch. (10)

Rnd 2: 2 sc in next st, sc in next 2 sts, 2 sc in next 3 sts, sc in next 2 sts, 2 sc in next 2 sts. (16)

Rnd 3: Sc in next st, 2 sc in next st, sc in next 3 sts, 2 sc in next st, (sc in next st, 2 sc in next st) 2 times, sc in next 3 sts, 2 sc in next st, sc in next st, 2 sc in next st. (22)

Rnd 4: Working in back loops only. Sc in each st around. (22)

Rnd 5: Sc in next 6 sts, (sc next 2 sts tog) 3 times, sc in next 10 sts. (19)

Rnd 6: Sc in next 5 sts, (sc next 2 sts tog) 3 times, sc in next 8 sts, changing to **ICE BLUE** in last 2 loops of last st. (16)

Rnd 7: (Sc in next 2 sts, sc next 2 sts tog) 4 times. (12) Stuff foot.

Rnd 8-12: Sc in each st around. (12)

Rnd 13: Sc in each st around, fasten off. (12)

Body

Rnd 1: With **ICE BLUE**, hold legs together with upper inner thighs together. Insert hook in the center on innermost thigh of **FIRST LEG**, pull out the loop from **SECOND LEG**, ch 1, sc in same st (Do not count this stitch, it is only for connecting legs together.), (2 sc in next st, sc in next 10 sts) on **SECOND LEG** (mark first st), (2 sc in next st, sc in next 10 sts) on **FIRST LEG**. (24)

Rnd 2: (Sc in next 2 sts, 2 sc in next st) 8 times. Stuff legs. (32)

Rnd 3: Sc in each st around. (32)

Rnd 4: (Sc in next 7 sts, 2 sc in next st) 4 times. (36)

Rnd 5: Sc in each st around. (36)

Rnd 6: Working in back loops only. Sc in each st around. (36)

Rnd 7: (Sc next 2 sts tog, sc in next 7 sts) 4 times. (32)

Rnd 8: Sc in each st around. (32)

Rnd 9: Sc in next 3 sts, sc next 2 sts tog, (sc in next 6 sts, sc next 2 sts tog) 3 times, sc in next 3 sts. (28)

Rnd 10: Sc in each st around. (28)

Rnd 11: (Sc next 2 sts tog, sc in next 5 sts) 4 times. (24)

Rnd 12: Sc in each st around. (24)

Rnd 13: Sc in next 2 sts, sc next 2 sts tog, (sc in next 4 sts, sc next 2 sts tog) 3 times, sc in next 2 sts. (20)

Rnd 14: Sc in each st around. (20)

Rnd 15: (Sc next 2 sts tog, sc in next 3 sts) 4 times. (16)

Rnd 16: Sc in each st around. (16)

Rnd 17: (Sc next 2 sts tog, sc in next 2 sts) 4 times. Leave long end for sewing, fasten off. (12)

Edge of Shirt

Rnd 1: Working in front loops of round 5 of the body and head pointed towards you. With **ICE BLUE**, join with sl st, ch 1, sc in same st, sc in each st around. (36)

Rnd 2: Sc in each st around, join with sl st in first st. Fasten off.

Arm

Make 2 and only stuff hands.

Rnd 1: With **BROWN**, 6 sc in a magic ring. (6)

Rnd 2: (Sc in next st, 2 sc in next st) 3 times. (9)

Rnd 3: Sc in each st around. (9)

Rnd 4: (Sc next 2 sts tog, sc in next st) 3 times, changing to **WHITE** in last 2 loops of last st. (6) Stuff hand.

Rnd 5-14: Sc in each st around. (6)

Rnd 15: Sc in each st around, sl st to the first st, leave long end for sewing, fasten off. (6)

Gown

Working in rows.

Row 1: With **WHITE**, ch 17, sc in second ch from hook, sc in 15 chs, turn. (16)

Row 2: Ch 1, 2 sc in first st, (sc in next 4 sts, 2 sc in next st) 3 times, turn. (20)

Row 3: Ch 1, sc in each st, turn. (20)

Row 4: Ch 1, 2 sc in first st, sc in next 5 sts, 2 sc in next st, sc in next 6 sts, 2 sc in next st, sc in next 5 sts, 2 sc in next st, turn. (24)

Row 5: Ch 1, sc in each st, turn. (24)

Row 6: Ch 1, 2 sc in first st, sc in next 7 sts, 2 sc in next st, sc in next 6 sts, 2 sc in next st, sc in next 7 sts, 2 sc in next st, turn. (28)

Row 7: Ch 1, sc in each st, turn. (28)

Row 8: Ch 1, 2 sc in first st, sc in next 8 sts, 2 sc in next st, sc in next 8 sts, 2 sc in next st, sc in next 8 sts, 2 sc in next st, turn. (32)

Row 9: Ch 1, sc in each st, turn. (32)

Row 10: Ch 1, 2 sc in first st, sc in next 9 sts, 2 sc in next st, sc in next 10 sts, 2 sc in next st, sc in next 9 sts, 2 sc in next st, turn. (36)

Row 11: Ch 1, sc in each st, turn. (36)

Row 12: Ch 1, sc in next 17 sts, 2 sc in next 2 sts, sc in next 17 sts, turn. (38)

Row 13-18: Ch 1, sc in each st, turn. (38)

Row 19: Ch 1, sc in each st to the end of row then sc around the edge, fasten off.

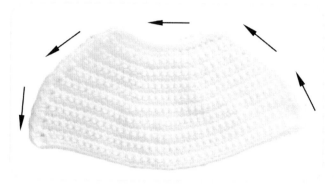

Pocket

Make 2.

Working in rows.

Row 1: With **WHITE**, ch 6, sc in second ch from hook, sc in 4 chs, turn. (5)

Row 2-3: Ch 1, sc in each st, turn. (5)

Row 4: Ch 1, sc in each st, fasten off.

Head

For the bear's head: see page 35.

Finishing

- Sew head to the body.
- Wrap gown around the body and use pins to hold it in place.
- Sew arms to the body.
- Sew pockets on both front sides of gown.

NURSE

Leg

Make 2.

Start by crocheting sc around the foundation chain:

Rnd 1: With **WHITE**, ch 5, sc in second chain from hook, sc in next 2 chs, 3 sc in last ch; working in remaining loops on opposite side of chain, sc in next 2 chs, 2 sc in next ch. (10)

Rnd 2: 2 sc in next st, sc in next 2 sts, 2 sc in next 3 sts, sc in next 2 sts, 2 sc in next 2 sts. (16)

Rnd 3: Sc in next st, 2 sc in next st, sc in next 3 sts, 2 sc in next st, (sc in next st, 2 sc in next st) 2 times, sc in next 3 sts, 2 sc in next st, sc in next st, 2 sc in next st. (22)

Rnd 4: Working in back loops only. Sc in each st around. (22)

Rnd 5: Sc in next 6 sts, (sc next 2 sts tog) 3 times, sc in next 10 sts. (19)

Rnd 6: Sc in next 5 sts, (sc next 2 sts tog) 3 times, sc in next 8 sts, changing to **YELLOW** in last 2 loops of last st. (16)

Rnd 7: Working in back loops only. (Sc in next 2 sts, sc next 2 sts tog) 4 times. (12) Stuff foot.

Rnd 8-12: Sc in each st around. (12)

Rnd 13: Sc in each st around, fasten off. (12)

Body

Rnd 1: With **WHITE**, hold legs together with upper inner thighs together. Insert hook in the center on innermost thigh of first leg, pull out the loop from second leg, ch 1, sc in same st (Do not count this stitch, it is only for connecting legs together.), (2 sc in next st, sc in next 10 sts) on second leg (mark first st), (2 sc in next st, sc in next 10 sts) on first leg. (24)

Rnd 2: (Sc in next 2 sts, 2 sc in next st) 8 times. Stuff legs. (32)

Rnd 3: Sc in each st around. (32)

Rnd 4: (Sc in next 7 sts, 2 sc in next st) 4 times. (36)

Rnd 5: Sc in each st around. (36)

Rnd 6: Working in back loops only. Sc in each st around. (36)

Rnd 7: (Sc next 2 sts tog, sc in next 7 sts) 4 times. (32)

Rnd 8: Sc in each st around. (32)

Rnd 9: Sc in next 3 sts, sc next 2 sts tog, (sc in next 6 sts, sc next 2 sts tog) 3 times, sc in next 3 sts. (28)

Rnd 10: Sc in each st around. (28)

Rnd 11: (Sc next 2 sts tog, sc in next 5 sts) 4 times. (24)

Rnd 12: Sc in each st around. (24)

Rnd 13: Sc in next 2 sts, sc next 2 sts tog, (sc in next 4 sts, sc next 2 sts tog) 3 times, sc in next 2 sts. (20)

Rnd 14: Sc in each st around. (20)

Rnd 15: (Sc next 2 sts tog, sc in next 3 sts) 4 times. (16)

Rnd 16: Sc in each st around. (16)

Rnd 17: (Sc next 2 sts tog, sc in next 2 sts) 4 times. Leave long end for sewing, fasten off. (12)

Skirt

Rnd 1: Working in front loops of round 5 of the body and head pointed towards you. With **WHITE**, join with sl st, ch 1, sc in same st, sc in each st around. (36)

Rnd 2: (Sc in next 11 sts, 2 sc in next st) 3 times. (39)

Rnd 3-6: Sc in each st around. (39)

Rnd 7: Sc in each st around, join with sl st in first st. Fasten off.

Arm

Make 2 and only stuff hands.

Rnd 1: With **YELLOW**, 6 sc in a magic ring. (6)

Rnd 2: (Sc in next st, 2 sc in next st) 3 times. (9)

Rnd 3: Sc in each st around. (9)

Rnd 4: (Sc in next st, sc next 2 sts tog) 3 times. (6)
Stuff hand.

Rnd 5-10: Sc in each st around. (6)

Rnd 11: Sc in each st around, changing to **WHITE** in last 2 loops of last st. (6)

Rnd 12-14: Sc in each st around. (6)

Rnd 15: Sc in each st around, sl st to the first st, leave long end for sewing, fasten off. (6)

Nurse Cap

Working in rows.

Row 1: With **WHITE**, ch 16, sc in second chain from hook, sc in each chain across, turn. (15)

Row 2: Ch 1, sc in each st across, turn. (15)

Row 3: Working in back loops only. Ch 1, sc in each st across, turn. (15)

Row 4: Ch 1, sc in each st across, fasten off. (15)

Row 5: Middle Part, join to the 5th st on row 4, ch 1, sc in next 7 sts, turn. (7)

Row 6: Ch 1, sc in each st across, turn. (7)

Row 7: Ch 1, sc first 2 sts tog, sc in next 3 sts, sc next 2 sts tog, leave long end for sewing, fasten off. (5)
Sew edge 1 to edge 2 and sew edge 3 to edge 4.

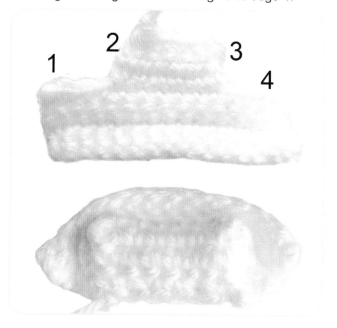

Collar

WHITE color, see page 30.

Head & Tail

For the cat's head and tail: see page 35.

Finishing

- Sew head to the body.
- Sew arms to the body.
- Sew tail on rnds 6-7, middle back of the body.
- Wrap collar around the neck and sew.
- Put the nurse cap on and sew to the head.

CHEF

Leg

Make 2.

Start by crocheting sc around the foundation chain:

Rnd 1: With **BLACK**, ch 5, sc in second chain from hook, sc in next 2 chs, 3 sc in last ch; working in remaining loops on opposite side of chain, sc in next 2 chs, 2 sc in next ch. (10)

Rnd 2: 2 sc in next st, sc in next 2 sts, 2 sc in next 3 sts, sc in next 2 sts, 2 sc in next 2 sts. (16)

Rnd 3: Sc in next st, 2 sc in next st, sc in next 3 sts, 2 sc in next st, (sc in next st, 2 sc in next st) 2 times, sc in next 3 sts, 2 sc in next st, sc in next st, 2 sc in next st. (22)

Rnd 4: Working in back loops only. Sc in each st around. (22)

Rnd 5: Sc in next 6 sts, (sc next 2 sts tog) 3 times, sc in next 10 sts. (19)

Rnd 6: Sc in next 5 sts, (sc next 2 sts tog) 3 times, sc in next 8 sts. (16)

Rnd 7: (Sc in next 2 sts, sc next 2 sts tog) 4 times. (12) Stuff foot.

Rnd 8-12: Sc in each st around. (12)

Rnd 13: Sc in each st around, fasten off. (12)

Body

Rnd 1: With **BLACK**, hold legs together with upper inner thighs together. Insert hook in the center on innermost thigh of first leg, pull out the loop from second leg, ch 1, sc in same st (Do not count this stitch, it is only for connecting legs together.), (2 sc in next st, sc in next 10 sts) on second leg (mark first st), (2 sc in next st, sc in next 10 sts) on first leg. (24)

Rnd 2: (Sc in next 2 sts, 2 sc in next st) 8 times. Stuff legs. (32)

Rnd 3: Sc in each st around. (32)

Rnd 4: (Sc in next 7 sts, 2 sc in next st) 4 times, changing to **WHITE** in last 2 loops of last st. (36)

Rnd 5: Sc in each st around. (36)

Rnd 6: Working in back loops only. Sc in each st around. (36)

Rnd 7: (Sc next 2 sts tog, sc in next 7 sts) 4 times. (32)

Rnd 8: Sc in each st around. (32)

Rnd 9: Sc in next 3 sts, sc next 2 sts tog, (sc in next 6 sts, sc next 2 sts tog) 3 times, sc in next 3 sts. (28)

Rnd 10: Sc in each st around. (28)

Rnd 11: (Sc next 2 sts tog, sc in next 5 sts) 4 times. (24)

Rnd 12: Sc in each st around. (24)

Rnd 13: Sc in next 2 sts, sc next 2 sts tog, (sc in next 4 sts, sc next 2 sts tog) 3 times, sc in next 2 sts. (20)

Rnd 14: Sc in each st around. (20)

Rnd 15: (Sc next 2 sts tog, sc in next 3 sts) 4 times. (16)

Rnd 16: Sc in each st around. (16)

Rnd 17: (Sc next 2 sts tog, sc in next 2 sts) 4 times. Leave long end for sewing, fasten off. (12)

Edge of Shirt

Rnd 1: Working in front loops of round 5 of the body and head pointed towards you. With **WHITE**, join with sl st, ch 1, sc in same st, sc in each st around. (36)

Rnd 2: Sc in each st around, join with sl st in first st. Fasten off.

Arm

Make 2 and only stuff hands.

Rnd 1: With **LIGHT PINK**, 6 sc in a magic ring. (6)

Rnd 2: (Sc in next st, 2 sc in next st) 3 times. (9)

Rnd 3: Sc in each st around. (9)

Rnd 4: (Sc next 2 sts tog, sc in next st) 3 times, changing to **WHITE** in last 2 loops of last st. (6) Stuff hand.

Rnd 5-14: Sc in each st around. (6)

Rnd 15: Sc in each st around, sl st to the first st, leave long end for sewing, fasten off. (6)

Hat

Rnd 1: With **WHITE**, 6 sc in a magic ring. (6)

Rnd 2: 2 sc in each st around. (12)

Rnd 3: (Sc in next st, 2 sc in next st) 6 times. (18)

Rnd 4: (2 sc in next st, sc in next 2 sts) 6 times. (24)

Rnd 5: (Sc in next 3 sts, 2 sc in next st) 6 times. (30)

Rnd 6: Sc in next 2 sts, 2 sc in next st, (sc in next 4 sts, 2 sc in next st) 5 times, sc in next 2 sts. (36)

Rnd 7: (Sc in next 5 sts, 2 sc in next st) 6 times. (42)

Rnd 8: Sc in next 3 sts, 2 sc in next st, (sc in next 6 sts, 2 sc in next st) 5 times, sc in next 3 sts. (48)

Rnd 9: (Sc in next 7 sts, 2 sc in next st) 6 times. (54)

Rnd 10: (Skip next 2 sts, sc in next 4 sts) 9 times. (36)

Rnd 11: (Skip next st, sc in next 3 sts) 9 times. (27)

Rnd 12: Sc in each st around. (27)

Rnd 13: Sc in each st around, sl st in first st, leave long end for sewing, fasten off. (27)

Scarf

Working in rows.

Row 1: With **RED**, ch 35, sc in second ch from hook, sc in next 33 chs, leave long end for sewing, fasten off. (34)

Head & Tail

For the pig's head and tail: see page 37.

Finishing

- Sew head to the body.
- Sew arms to the body.
- Sew tail on rnd 6 of the body.
- Pin the hat on middle top of head and sew. Stuff before sewing the opening closed.
- Tie scarf around neck.

POLICEMAN

Leg
Make 2.

Start by crocheting sc around the foundation chain:

Rnd 1: With **BLACK**, ch 5, sc in second chain from hook, sc in next 2 chs, 3 sc in last ch; working in remaining loops on opposite side of chain, sc in next 2 chs, 2 sc in next ch. (10)

Rnd 2: 2 sc in next st, sc in next 2 sts, 2 sc in next 3 sts, sc in next 2 sts, 2 sc in next 2 sts. (16)

Rnd 3: Sc in next st, 2 sc in next st, sc in next 3 sts, 2 sc in next st, (sc in next st, 2 sc in next st) 2 times, sc in next 3 sts, 2 sc in next st, sc in next st, 2 sc in next st. (22)

Rnd 4: Working in back loops only. Sc in each st around. (22)

Rnd 5: Sc in next 6 sts, (sc next 2 sts tog) 3 times, sc in next 10 sts. (19)

Rnd 6: Sc in next 5 sts, (sc next 2 sts tog) 3 times, sc in next 8 sts, changing to **MARINE** in last 2 loops of last st. (16)

Rnd 7: (Sc in next 2 sts, sc next 2 sts tog) 4 times. (12) Stuff foot.

Rnd 8-12: Sc in each st around. (12)

Rnd 13: Sc in each st around, fasten off. (12)

Body

Rnd 1: With **MARINE**, hold legs together with upper inner thighs together. Insert hook in the center on innermost thigh of first leg, pull out the loop from second leg, ch 1, sc in same st (Do not count this stitch, it is only for connecting legs together.), (2 sc in next st, sc in next 10 sts) on second leg (mark first st), (2 sc in next st, sc in next 10 sts) on first leg. (24)

Rnd 2: (Sc in next 2 sts, 2 sc in next st) 8 times. Stuff legs. (32)

Rnd 3: Sc in each st around. (32)

Rnd 4: (Sc in next 7 sts, 2 sc in next st) 4 times. (36)

Rnd 5-6: Sc in each st around. (36)

Rnd 7: (Sc next 2 sts tog, sc in next 7 sts) 4 times. (32)

Rnd 8: Sc in each st around. (32)

Rnd 9: Sc in next 3 sts, sc next 2 sts tog, (sc in next 6 sts, sc next 2 sts tog) 3 times, sc in next 3 sts. (28)

Rnd 10: Sc in each st around. (28)

Rnd 11: (Sc next 2 sts tog, sc in next 5 sts) 4 times. (24)

Rnd 12: Sc in each st around. (24)

Rnd 13: Sc in next 2 sts, sc next 2 sts tog, (sc in next 4 sts, sc next 2 sts tog) 3 times, sc in next 2 sts. (20)

Rnd 14: Sc in each st around. (20)

Rnd 15: (Sc next 2 sts tog, sc in next 3 sts) 4 times. (16)

Rnd 16: Sc in each st around. (16)

Rnd 17: (Sc next 2 sts tog, sc in next 2 sts) 4 times. Leave long end for sewing, fasten off. (12)

Arm
Make 2 and only stuff hands.

Rnd 1: With **ORANGE**, 6 sc in a magic ring. (6)

Rnd 2: (Sc in next st, 2 sc in next st) 3 times. (9)

Rnd 3: Sc in each st around. (9)

Rnd 4: (Sc next 2 sts tog, sc in next st) 3 times, changing to **MARINE** in last 2 loops of last st. (6) Stuff hand.

Rnd 5-14: Sc in each st around. (6)

Rnd 15: Sc in each st around, sl st to the first st, leave long end for sewing, fasten off. (6)

Tie

Rnd 1: With **BLACK**, 6 sc in a magic ring. (6)

Rnd 2: (2 sc in next st, sc in next st) 3 times. (9)

Rnd 3: (Sc next 2 sts tog, sc in next st) 3 times. (6)

Rnd 4: Sc next 2 sts tog, sc in next 4 sts. (5)

Rnd 5-6: Sc in each st around. (5)

Rnd 7: Sc in each st around, join with sl st in next st, leave long end for sewing, fasten off.

Hat

Rnd 1: With **MARINE**, 6 sc in a magic ring. (6)

Rnd 2: 2 sc in each st around. (12)

Rnd 3: (Sc in next st, 2 sc in next st) 6 times. (18)

Rnd 4: (Sc in next 2 sts, 2 sc in next st) 6 times. (24)

Rnd 5: (Sc in next 3 sts, 2 sc in next st) 6 times. (30)

Rnd 6: (Sc in next 4 sts, 2 sc in next st) 6 times. (36)

Rnd 7: (Sc in next 5 sts, 2 sc in next st) 6 times. (42)

Rnd 8: (Sc in next 6 sts, 2 sc in next st) 6 times. (48)

Rnd 9: Working in back loops only. (Sc in next 6 sts, sc next 2 sts tog) 6 times. (42)

Rnd 10: Sc in each st around. (42)

Rnd 11: (Sc in next 5 sts, sc next 2 sts tog) 6 times. (36)

Rnd 12: Sc in each st around, changing to **BLACK** in last 2 loops of last st. (36)

Rnd 13: Sc in each st around. (36)

Rnd 14: Visor: sc in next st, 2 hdc in next 11 sts, sc in next st, sl st in next st, leave long end for sewing, fasten off. (24)

Badge

Working in rows.

Row 1: With **YELLOW**, ch 4, sc in second chain from hook, sc in next 2 chs, turn. (3)

Row 2: Ch 1, sc in each st across, turn. (3)

Row 3: Ch 1, sc 3 sts tog, leave long end for sewing, fasten off. (1)

Sew badge in front of the hat.

Collar

MARINE, see page 30.

Belt

BLACK, see page 30.

Head & Tail

For the tiger's head and tail: see page 36.

For the cat's head and tail: see page 35.

Finishing

- Sew head to the body.
- Sew arms to the body.
- Sew belt on rnds 5-6 and use **YELLOW YARN** to embroider a buckle (see page 29).
- Sew a tie in the middle front of the body.
- Wrap collar around the neck and sew.
- Sew hat on top of the head, stuff the hat before sewing the opening closed.
- Sew tail on rnd 5 of the body.

FIREFIGHTER

Leg

Make 2.

Start by crocheting sc around the foundation chain:

Rnd 1: With **BLACK**, ch 5, sc in second chain from hook, sc in next 2 chs, 3 sc in last ch; working in remaining loops on opposite side of chain, sc in next 2 chs, 2 sc in next ch. (10)

Rnd 2: 2 sc in next st, sc in next 2 sts, 2 sc in next 3 sts, sc in next 2 sts, 2 sc in next 2 sts. (16)

Rnd 3: Sc in next st, 2 sc in next st, sc in next 3 sts, 2 sc in next st, (sc in next st, 2 sc in next st) 2 times, sc in next 3 sts, 2 sc in next st, sc in next st, 2 sc in next st. (22)

Rnd 4: Working in back loops only. Sc in each st around. (22)

Rnd 5: Sc in next 6 sts, (sc next 2 sts tog) 3 times, sc in next 10 sts. (19)

Rnd 6: Sc in next 5 sts, (sc next 2 sts tog) 3 times, sc in next 8 sts, changing to **RED** in last 2 loops of last st. (16)

Rnd 7: (Sc in next 2 sts, sc next 2 sts tog) 4 times. (12) Stuff foot.

Rnd 8: Sc in each st around, changing to **YELLOW** in last 2 loops of last st. (12)

Rnd 9: Sc in each st around, changing to **RED** in last 2 loops of last st. (12)

52

Rnd 10-12: Sc in each st around. (12)

Rnd 13: Sc in each st around, fasten off. (12)

Body

Rnd 1: With **RED**, hold legs together with upper inner thighs together. Insert hook in the center on innermost thigh of **FIRST LEG**, pull out the loop from **SECOND LEG**, ch 1, sc in same st (Do not count this stitch, it is only for connecting legs together.), (2 sc in next st, sc in next 10 sts) on **SECOND LEG** (mark first st), (2 sc in next st, sc in next 10 sts) on **FIRST LEG**. (24)

Rnd 2: (Sc in next 2 sts, 2 sc in next st) 8 times. Stuff legs. (32)

Rnd 3: Sc in each st around. (32)

Rnd 4: (Sc in next 7 sts, 2 sc in next st) 4 times. (36)

Rnd 5: Sc in each st around, changing to **YELLOW** in last 2 loops of last st. (36)

Rnd 6: Working in back loops only. Sc in each st around, changing to **RED** in last 2 loops of last st. (36)

Rnd 7: (Sc next 2 sts tog, sc in next 7 sts) 4 times. (32)

Rnd 8: Sc in each st around. (32)

Rnd 9: Sc in next 3 sts, sc next 2 sts tog, (sc in next 6 sts, sc next 2 sts tog) 3 times, sc in next 3 sts. (28)

Rnd 10: Sc in each st around. (28)

Rnd 11: (Sc next 2 sts tog, sc in next 5 sts) 4 times. (24)

Rnd 12: Sc in each st around. (24)

Rnd 13: Sc in next 2 sts, sc next 2 sts tog, (sc in next 4 sts, sc next 2 sts tog) 3 times, sc in next 2 sts, changing to **YELLOW** in last 2 loops of last st. (20)

Rnd 14: Sc in each st around, changing to **RED** in last 2 loops of last st. (20)

Rnd 15: (Sc next 2 sts tog, sc in next 3 sts) 4 times. (16)

Rnd 16: Sc in each st around. (16)

Rnd 17: (Sc next 2 sts tog, sc in next 2 sts) 4 times. Leave long end for sewing, fasten off. (12)

Edge of Shirt

Rnd 1: Working in front loops of round 5 of the body and head pointed towards you. With **RED**, join with sl st, ch 1, sc in same st, sc in each st around. (36)

Rnd 2: Sc in each st around, join with sl st in first st. Fasten off.

Arm

Make 2 and only stuff hands.

Rnd 1: With **GREY**, 6 sc in a magic ring. (6)

Rnd 2: (Sc in next st, 2 sc in next st) 3 times. (9)

Rnd 3: Sc in each st around. (9)

Rnd 4: (Sc next 2 sts tog, sc in next st) 3 times, changing to **RED** in last 2 loops of last st. (6) Stuff hand.

Rnd 5: Sc in each st around, changing to **YELLOW** in last 2 loops of last st. (6)

Rnd 6: Sc in each st around, changing to **RED** in last 2 loops of last st. (6)

Rnd 7-10: Sc in each st around. (6)

Rnd 11: Sc in each st around, changing to **YELLOW** in last 2 loops of last st. (6)

Rnd 12: Sc in each st around, changing to **RED** in last 2 loops of last st. (6)

Rnd 13-14: Sc in each st around. (6)

Rnd 15: Sc in each st around, sl st to the first st, leave long end for sewing, fasten off. (6)

Hat

Rnd 1: With **RED**, 6 sc in a magic ring. (6)

Rnd 2: 2 sc in each st around. (12)

Rnd 3: (Sc in next st, 2 sc in next st) 6 times. (18)

Rnd 4: (2 sc in next st, sc in next 2 sts) 6 times. (24)

Rnd 5: (Sc in next 3 sts, 2 sc in next st) 6 times. (30)

Rnd 6: Sc in next 2 sts, 2 sc in next st, (sc in next 4 sts, 2 sc in next st) 5 times, sc in next 2 sts. (36)

Rnd 7-10: Sc in each st around. (36)

Rnd 11: (Dc in next st, 2 dc in next st) 6 times, (sc in next st, 2 sc in next st) 12 times. (54)

Rnd 12: Sc in next 18 sts, sl st in next 36 sts, leave long end for sewing, fasten off. (54)

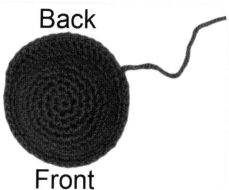

Back

Front

Badge

Working in rows.

Row 1: With **YELLOW**, ch 4, sc in second chain from hook, sc in next 2 chs, turn. (3)

Row 2: Ch 1, sc in each st across, turn. (3)

Row 3: Ch 1, sc 3 sts tog, leave long end for sewing, fasten off. (1)

Sew badge on the front of hat.

Collar

RED color, see page 30.

Head & Tail

For the elephant's head and tail: see page 38.

Finishing

- Sew head to the body.
- Sew arms to the body.
- Sew tail on rnd 6 of the body.
- Wrap collar around the neck and sew.
- Sew hat on top of the head, stuff the hat before sewing the opening closed.

SAILOR

Leg

Make 2.

Start by crocheting sc around the foundation chain:

Rnd 1: With **BLACK**, ch 5, sc in second chain from hook, sc in next 2 chs, 3 sc in last ch; working in remaining loops on opposite side of chain, sc in next 2 chs, 2 sc in next ch. (10)

Rnd 2: 2 sc in next st, sc in next 2 sts, 2 sc in next 3 sts, sc in next 2 sts, 2 sc in next 2 sts. (16)

Rnd 3: Sc in next st, 2 sc in next st, sc in next 3 sts, 2 sc in next st, (sc in next st, 2 sc in next st) 2 times, sc in next 3 sts, 2 sc in next st, sc in next st, 2 sc in next st. (22)

Rnd 4: Working in back loops only. Sc in each st around. (22)

Rnd 5: Sc in next 6 sts, (sc next 2 sts tog) 3 times, sc in next 10 sts. (19)

Rnd 6: Sc in next 5 sts, (sc next 2 sts tog) 3 times, sc in next 8 sts, changing to **WHITE** in last 2 loops of last st. (16)

Rnd 7: (Sc in next 2 sts, sc next 2 sts tog) 4 times. (12) Stuff foot.

Rnd 8-12: Sc in each st around. (12)

Rnd 13: Sc in each st around, fasten off. (12)

Body

Rnd 1: With **WHITE**, hold legs together with upper inner thighs together. Insert hook in the center on innermost thigh of **FIRST LEG**, pull out the loop from **SECOND LEG**, ch 1, sc in same st (Do not count this stitch, it is only for connecting legs together.), (2 sc in next st, sc in next 10 sts) on **SECOND LEG** (mark first st), (2 sc in next st, sc in next 10 sts) on **FIRST LEG**. (24)

Rnd 2: (Sc in next 2 sts, 2 sc in next st) 8 times. Stuff legs. (32)

Rnd 3: Sc in each st around. (32)

Rnd 4: (Sc in next 7 sts, 2 sc in next st) 4 times. (36)

Rnd 5: Sc in each st around. (36)

Rnd 6: Working in back loops only. Sc in each st around. (36)

Rnd 7: (Sc next 2 sts tog, sc in next 7 sts) 4 times. (32)

Rnd 8: Sc in each st around. (32)

Rnd 9: Sc in next 3 sts, sc next 2 sts tog, (sc in next 6 sts, sc next 2 sts tog) 3 times, sc in next 3 sts. (28)

Rnd 10: Sc in each st around. (28)

Rnd 11: (Sc next 2 sts tog, sc in next 5 sts) 4 times. (24)

Rnd 12: Sc in each st around. (24)

Rnd 13: Sc in next 2 sts, sc next 2 sts tog, (sc in next 4 sts, sc next 2 sts tog) 3 times, sc in next 2 sts. (20)

Rnd 14: Sc in each st around. (20)

Rnd 15: (Sc next 2 sts tog, sc in next 3 sts) 4 times. (16)

Rnd 16: Sc in each st around. (16)

Rnd 17: (Sc next 2 sts tog, sc in next 2 sts) 4 times. Leave long end for sewing, fasten off. (12)

Edge of Shirt

Rnd 1: Working in front loops of round 5 of the body and head pointed towards you. With **WHITE**, join with sl st, ch 1, sc in same st, sc in each st around. (36)

Rnd 2: Sc in each st around, join with sl st in first st. Fasten off.

Arm

Make 2 and only stuff hands.

Rnd 1: With **BROWN**, 6 sc in a magic ring. (6)

Rnd 2: (Sc in next st, 2 sc in next st) 3 times. (9)

Rnd 3: Sc in each st around. (9)

Rnd 4: (Sc next 2 sts tog, sc in next st) 3 times, changing to **WHITE** in last 2 loops of last st. (6) Stuff hand.

Rnd 5-14: Sc in each st around. (6)

Rnd 15: Sc in each st around, sl st to the first st, leave long end for sewing, fasten off. (6)

Hat

Rnd 1: With **WHITE**, 6 sc in a magic ring. (6)

Rnd 2: 2 sc in each st around. (12)

Rnd 3: (Sc in next st, 2 sc in next st) 6 times. (18)

Rnd 4: (2 sc in next st, sc in next 2 sts) 6 times. (24)

Rnd 5: (Sc in next 3 sts, 2 sc in next st) 6 times. (30)

Rnd 6: Sc in next 2 sts, 2 sc in next st, (sc in next 4 sts, 2 sc in next st) 5 times, sc in next 2 sts. (36)

Rnd 7: (Sc in next 5 sts, 2 sc in next st) 6 times. (42)

Rnd 8: Sc in next 3 sts, 2 sc in next st, (sc in next 6 sts, 2 sc in next st) 5 times, sc in next 3 sts. (48)

Rnd 9: (Sc in next 7 sts, 2 sc in next st) 6 times. (54)

Rnd 10-13: Sc in each st around. (54)

Rnd 14: Working in front loops only. Sc in next 4 sts, 2 sc in next st, (sc in next 8 sts, 2 sc in next st) 5 times, sc in next 4 sts. (60)

Rnd 15: (Sc in next 11 sts, 2 sc in next st) 5 times. (65)

Rnd 16: Sc in next 6 sts, 2 sc in next st, (sc in next 12 sts, 2 sc in next st) 4 times, sc in next 6 sts. (70)

Rnd 17: Sc in each st around, sl st to the first st, leave long end for sewing, fasten off. (70)

Collar

Working in rows.

Row 1: With **WHITE**, ch 13, sc in second chain from hook, sc in next 11 chs, turn. (12)

Row 2: Ch 1, sc in each st across, turn. (12)

Row 3: Ch 1, sc in each st across, fasten off. (12)

Row 4: With **WHITE**, ch 7, sc in next 12 sts on row 3, ch 8, turn.

Row 5: Sc in second ch from hook, sc in next 6 chs, skip next st, sc in next 10 sts, skip next st, sc in next 7 chs, fasten off.

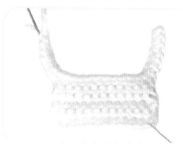

Row 6: With **MARINE BLUE**, ch 10, sl st around the outer edge of collar, ch 10, fasten off.

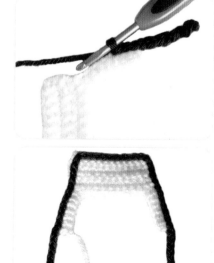

Head

For the dog's head: see page 39.

Finishing

- Sew head to the body.
- Sew arms to the body.
- Wrap collar around the neck, sew both **WHITE** ends together and tie the **BLUE** chains together.
- Put the hat on and sew to the head.

Small Hat

Rnd 1: With **WHITE**, 6 sc in a magic ring. (6)

Rnd 2: 2 sc in each st around. (12)

Rnd 3: (Sc in next st, 2 sc in next st) 6 times. (18)

Rnd 4: (2 sc in next st, sc in next 2 sts) 6 times. (24)

Rnd 5-7: Sc in each st around. (24)

Rnd 8: Working in front loops only. (Sc in next 3 sts, 2 sc in next st) 6 times. (30)

Rnd 9: Sc in each st around, sl st to the first st, leave long end for sewing, fasten off. (30)

FARMER

Leg

Make 2.

Start by crocheting sc around the foundation chain:

Rnd 1: With **DARK BROWN**, ch 5, sc in second chain from hook, sc in next 2 chs, 3 sc in last ch; working in remaining loops on opposite side of chain, sc in next 2 chs, 2 sc in next ch. (10)

Rnd 2: 2 sc in next st, sc in next 2 sts, 2 sc in next 3 sts, sc in next 2 sts, 2 sc in next 2 sts. (16)

Rnd 3: Sc in next st, 2 sc in next st, sc in next 3 sts, 2 sc in next st, (sc in next st, 2 sc in next st) 2 times, sc in next 3 sts, 2 sc in next st, sc in next st, 2 sc in next st. (22)

Rnd 4: Working in back loops only. Sc in each st around. (22)

Rnd 5: Sc in next 6 sts, (sc next 2 sts tog) 3 times, sc in next 10 sts. (19)

Rnd 6: Sc in next 5 sts, (sc next 2 sts tog) 3 times, sc in next 8 sts, changing to **MARINE** in last 2 loops of last st. (16)

Rnd 7: (Sc in next 2 sts, sc next 2 sts tog) 4 times. (12) Stuff foot.

Rnd 8-12: Sc in each st around. (12)

Rnd 13: Sc in each st around, fasten off. (12)

Body

Rnd 1: With **MARINE**, hold legs together with upper inner thighs together. Insert hook in the center on innermost thigh of first leg, pull out the loop from second leg, ch 1, sc in same st (Do not count this stitch, it is only for connecting legs together.), (2 sc in next st, sc in next 10 sts) on second leg (mark first st), (2 sc in next st, sc in next 10 sts) on first leg. (24)

Rnd 2: (Sc in next 2 sts, 2 sc in next st) 8 times. Stuff legs. (32)

Rnd 3: Sc in each st around. (32)

Rnd 4: (Sc in next 7 sts, 2 sc in next st) 4 times. (36)

Rnd 5-6: Sc in each st around. (36)

Rnd 7: (Sc next 2 sts tog, sc in next 7 sts) 4 times. (32)

Rnd 8: Sc in each st around. (32)

Rnd 9: Sc in next 3 sts, sc next 2 sts tog, (sc in next 6 sts, sc next 2 sts tog) 3 times, sc in next 3 sts, changing to **ORANGE** in last 2 loops of last st. (28)

Rnd 10: Working in back loops only. Sc in each st around. (28)

Rnd 11: (Sc next 2 sts tog, sc in next 5 sts) 4 times. (24)

Rnd 12: Sc in each st around. (24)

Rnd 13: Sc in next 2 sts, sc next 2 sts tog, (sc in next 4 sts, sc next 2 sts tog) 3 times, sc in next 2 sts. (20)

Rnd 14: Sc in each st around. (20)

Rnd 15: (Sc next 2 sts tog, sc in next 3 sts) 4 times. (16)

Rnd 16: Sc in each st around. (16)

Rnd 17: (Sc next 2 sts tog, sc in next 2 sts) 4 times. Leave long end for sewing, fasten off. (12)

Arm

Make 2 and only stuff hands.

Rnd 1: With **WHITE** (skin color), 6 sc in a magic ring. (6)

Rnd 2: (Sc in next st, 2 sc in next st) 3 times. (9)

Rnd 3: Sc in each st around. (9)

Rnd 4: (Sc next 2 sts tog, sc in next st) 3 times. (6) Stuff hand.

Rnd 5-10: Sc in each st around. (6)

Rnd 11: Sc in each st around, changing to **ORANGE** in last 2 loops of last st. (6)

Rnd 12-14: Sc in each st around. (6)

Rnd 15: Sc in each st around, sl st to the first st, leave long end for sewing, fasten off. (6)

Bib

Working in rows.

Row 1: With **MARINE**, ch 9, sc in second ch from hook, sc in next 7 sts, turn. (8)

Row 2: Ch 1, sc first 2 sts tog, sc in next 4 sts, sc next 2 sts tog, turn. (6)

Row 3: Ch 1, sc first 2 sts tog, sc in next 2 sts, sc next 2 sts tog, fasten off. (4)

Row 4: With **MARINE**, ch 12, sc in next 4 sts on row 3, ch 12, leave long end for sewing, fasten off.

Head & Tail

For the cow's head and tail: see page 42.
For the rabbit's head: see page 40.

Finishing

- Sew head to the body.
- Sew arms to the body.
- Pin bib to body and sew the first row of bib to free loops of rnd 9 of the body.

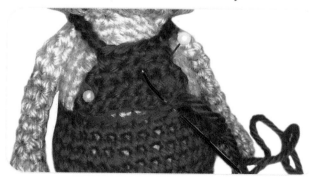

Cross the straps on the back and sew to the body.

For cow: sew tail on rnd 6 of the body.

BALLERINA

Leg

Make 2.

Start by crocheting sc around the foundation chain:

Rnd 1: With **WHITE**, ch 5, sc in second chain from hook, sc in next 2 chs, 3 sc in last ch; working in remaining loops on opposite side of chain, sc in next 2 chs, 2 sc in next ch. (10)

Rnd 2: 2 sc in next st, sc in next 2 sts, 2 sc in next 3 sts, sc in next 2 sts, 2 sc in next 2 sts. (16)

Rnd 3: Sc in next st, 2 sc in next st, sc in next 3 sts, 2 sc in next st, (sc in next st, 2 sc in next st) 2 times, sc in next 3 sts, 2 sc in next st, sc in next st, 2 sc in next st. (22)

Rnd 4: Working in back loops only. Sc in each st around. (22)

Rnd 5: Sc in next 6 sts, (sc next 2 sts tog) 3 times, sc in next 10 sts. (19)

Rnd 6: Sc in next 5 sts, (sc next 2 sts tog) 3 times, sc in next 8 sts, changing to **GREY** in last 2 loops of last st. (16)

Rnd 7: Working in back loops only. (Sc in next 2 sts, sc next 2 sts tog) 4 times. (12) Stuff foot.

Rnd 8-12: Sc in each st around. (12)

Rnd 13: Sc in each st around, fasten off. (12)

Body

Rnd 1: With **WHITE**, hold legs together with upper inner thighs together. Insert hook in the center on innermost thigh of first leg, pull out the loop from second leg, ch 1, sc in same st (Do not count this stitch, it is only for connecting legs together.), (2 sc in next st, sc in next 10 sts) on second leg (mark first st), (2 sc in next st, sc in next 10 sts) on first leg. (24)

Rnd 2: (Sc in next 2 sts, 2 sc in next st) 8 times. Stuff legs. (32)

Rnd 3: Sc in each st around. (32)

Rnd 4: (Sc in next 7 sts, 2 sc in next st) 4 times. (36)

Rnd 5: Sc in each st around. (36)

Rnd 6: Working in back loops only. Sc in each st around. (36)

Rnd 7: (Sc next 2 sts tog, sc in next 7 sts) 4 times. (32)

Rnd 8: Sc in each st around. (32)

Rnd 9: Sc in next 3 sts, sc next 2 sts tog, (sc in next 6 sts, sc next 2 sts tog) 3 times, sc in next 3 sts. (28)

Rnd 10: Sc in each st around. (28)

Rnd 11: (Sc next 2 sts tog, sc in next 5 sts) 4 times. (24)

Rnd 12: Sc in each st around. (24)

Rnd 13: Sc in next 2 sts, sc next 2 sts tog, (sc in next 4 sts, sc next 2 sts tog) 3 times, sc in next 2 sts. (20)

Rnd 14: Sc in each st around. (20)

Rnd 15: (Sc next 2 sts tog, sc in next 3 sts) 4 times. (16)

Rnd 16: Sc in each st around. (16)

Rnd 17: (Sc next 2 sts tog, sc in next 2 sts) 4 times. Leave long end for sewing, fasten off. (12)

Skirt

Rnd 1: Working in front loops of round 5 of the body and head pointed towards you. With **WHITE**, join with sl st, ch 1, sc in same st, sc in next 4 sts, 2 sc in next st, (sc in next 5 sts, 2 sc in next st) 5 times, sl st in first st. (42)

Rnd 2: Ch 3 (count as one dc), 2 dc in same st, 3 dc in next 41 sts, sl st in first st. (126)

Rnd 3: Ch 3 (count as one dc), dc in same st, 2 dc in next 125 sts, sl st in first st, fasten off. (252)

Arm

Make 2 and only stuff hands.

Rnd 1: With **GREY**, 6 sc in a magic ring. (6)

Rnd 2: (Sc in next st, 2 sc in next st) 3 times. (9)

Rnd 3: Sc in each st around. (9)

Rnd 4: (Sc in next st, sc next 2 sts tog) 3 times (6)
Stuff hand.

Rnd 5-14: Sc in each st around. (6)

Rnd 15: Sc in each st around, sl st to the first st, leave long end for sewing, fasten off. (6)

Head & Tail

For the mouse's head: see page 43.

For the rabbit's head: see page 40.

Finishing

- Sew head to the body.
- Sew arms to the body.
- Sew tail on rnd 6 of the body.

ENGINEER

Leg

Make 2.

Start by crocheting sc around the foundation chain:

Rnd 1: With **BLACK**, ch 5, sc in second chain from hook, sc in next 2 chs, 3 sc in last ch; working in remaining loops on opposite side of chain, sc in next 2 chs, 2 sc in next ch. (10)

Rnd 2: 2 sc in next st, sc in next 2 sts, 2 sc in next 3 sts, sc in next 2 sts, 2 sc in next 2 sts. (16)

Rnd 3: Sc in next st, 2 sc in next st, sc in next 3 sts, 2 sc in next st, (sc in next st, 2 sc in next st) 2 times, sc in next 3 sts, 2 sc in next st, sc in next st, 2 sc in next st. (22)

Rnd 4: Working in back loops only. Sc in each st around. (22)

Rnd 5: Sc in next 6 sts, (sc next 2 sts tog) 3 times, sc in next 10 sts. (19)

Rnd 6: Sc in next 5 sts, (sc next 2 sts tog) 3 times, sc in next 8 sts, changing to **MARINE** in last 2 loops of last st. (16)

Rnd 7: (Sc in next 2 sts, sc next 2 sts tog) 4 times. (12) Stuff foot.

Rnd 8-12: Sc in each st around. (12)

Rnd 13: Sc in each st around, fasten off. (12)

Body

Rnd 1: With **MARINE**, hold legs together with upper inner thighs together. Insert hook in the center on innermost thigh of **FIRST LEG**, pull out the loop from **SECOND LEG**, ch 1, sc in same st (Do not count this stitch, it is only for connecting legs together.), (2 sc in next st, sc in next 10 sts) on **SECOND LEG** (mark first st), (2 sc in next st, sc in next 10 sts) on **FIRST LEG**. (24)

Rnd 2: (Sc in next 2 sts, 2 sc in next st) 8 times. Stuff legs. (32)

Rnd 3: Sc in each st around. (32)

Rnd 4: (Sc in next 7 sts, 2 sc in next st) 4 times. (36)

Rnd 5: Sc in each st around, changing to **LIGHT BLUE** in last 2 loops of last st. (36)

Rnd 6: Sc in each st around. (36)

Rnd 7: (Sc next 2 sts tog, sc in next 7 sts) 4 times. (32)

Rnd 8: Sc in each st around. (32)

Rnd 9: Sc in next 3 sts, sc next 2 sts tog, (sc in next 6 sts, sc next 2 sts tog) 3 times, sc in next 3 sts. (28)

Rnd 10: Sc in each st around. (28)

Rnd 11: (Sc next 2 sts tog, sc in next 5 sts) 4 times. (24)

Rnd 12: Sc in each st around. (24)

Rnd 13: Sc in next 2 sts, sc next 2 sts tog, (sc in next 4 sts, sc next 2 sts tog) 3 times, sc in next 2 sts. (20)

Rnd 14: Sc in each st around. (20)

Rnd 15: (Sc next 2 sts tog, sc in next 3 sts) 4 times. (16)

Rnd 16: Sc in each st around. (16)

Rnd 17: (Sc next 2 sts tog, sc in next 2 sts) 4 times. Leave long end for sewing, fasten off. (12)

Arm

Make 2 and only stuff hands.

Rnd 1: With **BROWN**, 6 sc in a magic ring. (6)

Rnd 2: (Sc in next st, 2 sc in next st) 3 times. (9)

Rnd 3: Sc in each st around. (9)

Rnd 4: (Sc next 2 sts tog, sc in next st) 3 times, changing to **LIGHT BLUE** in last 2 loops of last st. (6) Stuff hand.

Rnd 5-14: Sc in each st around. (6)

Rnd 15: Sc in each st around, sl st to the first st, leave long end for sewing, fasten off. (6)

Belt

BLACK, see page 30.

Tie

Rnd 1: With **MARINE**, 6 sc in a magic ring. (6)

Rnd 2: (2 sc in next st, sc in next st) 3 times. (9)

Rnd 3: (Sc next 2 sts tog, sc in next st) 3 times. (6)

Rnd 4: Sc next 2 sts tog, sc in next 4 sts. (5)

Rnd 5-6: Sc in each st around. (5)

Rnd 7: Sc in each st around, join with sl st in next st, leave long end for sewing, fasten off.

Collar

LIGHT BLUE, see page 30.

Head & Tail

For the monkey's head and tail: see page 41.

Hat

Rnd 1: With **YELLOW**, 6 sc in a magic ring. (6)

Rnd 2: 2 sc in each st around. (12)

Rnd 3: (Sc in next st, 2 sc in next st) 6 times. (18)

Rnd 4: (2 sc in next st, sc in next 2 sts) 6 times. (24)

Rnd 5: (Sc in next 3 sts, 2 sc in next st) 6 times. (30)

Rnd 6: Sc in next 2 sts, 2 sc in next st, (sc in next 4 sts, 2 sc in next st) 5 times, sc in next 2 sts. (36)

Rnd 7-10: Sc in each st around. (36)

Rnd 11: Working in front loops only. Hdc in next st, 2 hdc in next st, (dc in next st, 2 dc in next st) 4 times, 2 hdc in next st, hdc in next st, sl st in next 24 sts, leave long end for sewing, fasten off. (42)

Finishing

- Sew head to the body.
- Sew arms to the body.
- Sew the tie in the middle front of the body.
- Wrap collar around the neck and sew.
- Sew hat on top of the head, stuff the hat before sewing the opening closed.
- Sew tail on the back of body below the belt.

TEACHER

Leg

Make 2.

Start by crocheting sc around the foundation chain:

Rnd 1: With **GREY**, ch 5, sc in second chain from hook, sc in next 2 chs, 3 sc in last ch; working in remaining loops on opposite side of chain, sc in next 2 chs, 2 sc in next ch. (10)

Rnd 2: 2 sc in next st, sc in next 2 sts, 2 sc in next 3 sts, sc in next 2 sts, 2 sc in next 2 sts. (16)

Rnd 3: Sc in next st, 2 sc in next st, sc in next 3 sts, 2 sc in next st, (sc in next st, 2 sc in next st) 2 times, sc in next 3 sts, 2 sc in next st, sc in next st, 2 sc in next st. (22)

Rnd 4: Working in back loops only. Sc in each st around. (22)

Rnd 5: Sc in next 6 sts, (sc next 2 sts tog) 3 times, sc in next 10 sts. (19)

Rnd 6: Sc in next 5 sts, (sc next 2 sts tog) 3 times, sc in next 8 sts, changing to **WHITE** in last 2 loops of last st. (16)

Rnd 7: Working in back loops only. (Sc in next 2 sts, sc next 2 sts tog) 4 times. (12) Stuff foot.

Rnd 8-12: Sc in each st around. (12)

Rnd 13: Sc in each st around, fasten off. (12)

Body

Rnd 1: With **LIGHT PINK**, hold legs together with upper inner thighs together. Insert hook in the center on innermost thigh of first leg, pull out the loop from second leg, ch 1, sc in same st (Do not count this stitch, it is only for connecting legs together.), (2 sc in next st, sc in next 10 sts) on second leg (mark first st), (2 sc in next st, sc in next 10 sts) on first leg. (24)

Rnd 2: (Sc in next 2 sts, 2 sc in next st) 8 times. Stuff legs. (32)

Rnd 3: Sc in each st around. (32)

Rnd 4: (Sc in next 7 sts, 2 sc in next st) 4 times. (36)

Rnd 5: Sc in each st around. (36)

Rnd 6: Working in back loops only. Sc in each st around. (36)

Rnd 7: (Sc next 2 sts tog, sc in next 7 sts) 4 times. (32)

Rnd 8: Sc in each st around. (32)

Rnd 9: Sc in next 3 sts, sc next 2 sts tog, (sc in next 6 sts, sc next 2 sts tog) 3 times, sc in next 3 sts. (28)

Rnd 10: Sc in each st around. (28)

Rnd 11: (Sc next 2 sts tog, sc in next 5 sts) 4 times. (24)

Rnd 12: Sc in each st around. (24)

Rnd 13: Sc in next 2 sts, sc next 2 sts tog, (sc in next 4 sts, sc next 2 sts tog) 3 times, sc in next 2 sts. (20)

Rnd 14: Sc in each st around. (20)

Rnd 15: (Sc next 2 sts tog, sc in next 3 sts) 4 times. (16)

Rnd 16: Sc in each st around. (16)

Rnd 17: (Sc next 2 sts tog, sc in next 2 sts) 4 times. Leave long end for sewing, fasten off. (12)

Skirt

Rnd 1: Working in front loops of round 5 of the body and head pointed towards you. With **DARK PINK**, join with sl st, ch 1, sc in same st, sc in each st around. (36)

Rnd 2: (Sc in next 11 sts, 2 sc in next st) 3 times. (39)

Rnd 3-6: Sc in each st around. (39)

Rnd 7: Sc in each st around, join with sl st in first st. Fasten off.

Arm

Make 2 and only stuff hands.

Rnd 1: With **WHITE**, 6 sc in a magic ring. (6)

Rnd 2: (Sc in next st, 2 sc in next st) 3 times. (9)

Rnd 3: Sc in each st around. (9)

Rnd 4: (Sc next 2 sts tog, sc in next st) 3 times, changing to **DARK PINK** in last 2 loops of last st. (6) Stuff hand.

Rnd 5-14: Sc in each st around. (6)

Rnd 15: Sc in each st around, sl st to the first st, leave long end for sewing, fasten off. (6)

Jacket

Working in rows.

Row 1: With **DARK PINK**, ch 17, sc in second ch from hook, sc in 15 chs, turn. (16)

Row 2: Ch 1, 2 sc in next st, (sc in next 4 sts, 2 sc in next st) 3 times, turn. (20)

Row 3: Ch 1, sc in each st, turn. (20)

Row 4: Ch 1, 2 sc in first st, sc in next 5 sts, 2 sc in next st, sc in next 6 sts, 2 sc in next st, sc in next 5 sts, 2 sc in next st, turn. (24)

Row 5: Ch 1, sc in each st, turn. (24)

Row 6: Ch 1, 2 sc in first st, sc in next 7 sts, 2 sc in next st, sc in next 6 sts, 2 sc in next st, sc in next 7 sts, 2 sc in next st, turn. (28)

Row 7: Ch 1, sc in each st, turn. (28)

Row 8: Ch 1, 2 sc in first st, sc in next 8 sts, 2 sc in next st, sc in next 8 sts, 2 sc in next st, sc in next 8 sts, 2 sc in next st, turn. (32)

Row 9: Ch 1, sc in each st, turn. (32)

Row 10: Ch 1, 2 sc in first st, sc in next 9 sts, 2 sc in next st, sc in next 10 sts, 2 sc in next st, sc in next 9 sts, 2 sc in next st, turn. (36)

Row 11: Ch 1, sc in each st, turn. (36)

Row 12: Ch 1, sc in next 17 sts, 2 sc in next 2 sts, sc in next 17 sts, turn. (38)

Row 13: Ch 1, sc in each st, turn. (38)

Row 14: Ch 1, sc in each st to the end of row then sc around the edge, fasten off.

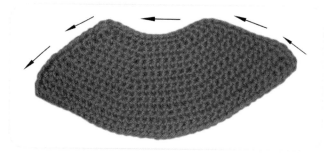

Head

For the rabbit's head: see page 40.

Finishing

- Sew head to the body.
- Wrap gown around the body and use pins to hold it in place.
- Sew arms to the body.

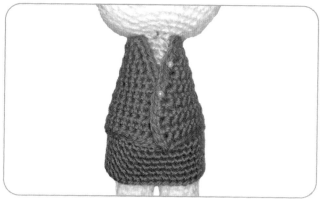

63

COPYRIGHT

First Edition
ISBN: 978-1-910407-82-0
Date of publication: December 12th 2020
Editor: Robert Appelboom
Book & Cover design, Patterns, Photographs and Illustrations : Sayjai Thawornsupacharoen
Publisher: K and J Publishing, 16 Whitegate Close, Swavesey, CB24 4TT

Thank you for supporting an independent designer.
Write to Sayjai : kandjdolls@gmail.com
kandjdolls.blogspot.com / www.facebook.com/kandjdolls.amigurumi.patterns

NOTES

Printed in Great Britain
by Amazon